COOL FIRE

A BLACK MAN'S POETIC ODYSSEY

Robert L. Dortch, Jr.

Copyright © 2025 by Robert Dortch, Jr.
All rights reserved
Printed and Bound in the United States of America

Published by
Jordan Sydnor Literary House
Email: info@thecoolfire.com
Website: thecoolfire.com

Interior photographs, courtesy of Robert Dortch, Jr.
Cover Design by David Landis
Interior design by Jessica Tilles/TWA Solutions.com
First printing May 2025
ISBN: 979-8-9988768-0-6

No part of this book may be reproduced, stored in a retrieval system or transmitted in any form or by any means without the prior written permission of the publisher—except by a reviewer who may quote brief passages in a review to be printed in a newspaper, magazine or journal.

For inquiry contact info@thecoolfire.com.

For Henry and Thelma Towns, James and Lucy Dortch, Price and Barbara Rogers, Reverend Robert C. Davis and Joel Blunk. The spirit of your legacy and love inspires me every day.

For my sons and future generations—may you grow in faith, rise boldly, dream freely, and live in your purpose.

TABLE OF CONTENTS

Prelude to the Odyssey vii

Chapter 1: In Search of Me
    When I Hear the Voice of Baldwin 1
    Getting to Know Me 5
    I AM 10
    Hoods, Hoodies, & Hope 13
    Pharaoh's Lost Child 15

Chapter 2: When I Speak of Intimacy
    Independent Love 21
    Misfits Longing 23
    Pastoral Erotic 25
    When the Stars See Love 27

Chapter 3: In the Spirit
    Inside the Silent Mind 31
    A Soul In Search of... 34
    Spiritual Tenacity 36
    Man's Mystery 39
    Just Before Morning 43
    Silent Joy 45

Chapter 4: In My Feelings
    A Q&A About Love 49
    Imperfectly Beautiful 51
    My Dear Friend 56
    Night Visits 60
    Strangers Overnight 64
    When Love Expires 68

Chapter 5: Can You Hear Me? 73
    When Will Tomorrow Come? 78
    A Moment in Harlem 81
    We Are They 83
    Tiki Torches & The Talented 10th 85
    Life. Breath. Death in 8:46 88
    Again 91
    American Prey 93
    Griots 98
    We Still Believe 101
    Can I Let You In? 106

Chapter 6: My Dreams
    Sacred Showers 106
    Make Time for Mornings Like This 109
    They Will Want to Know 111
    Not Just Another Morning 113
    Life 116
    Queen Becoming 119

Chapter 7: What's On My Mind
    Becoming Like You 123
    Gift of Knowing 127
    When Brothers Cry 131
    Falling In Love With You 133
    When We Fly 137

    In Gratitude 139

    About the Author 144

Prelude to the Odyssey

What does it mean to be a Black man? Since taking my first breath outside my mother's womb, my journey as a Black man has been a complicated odyssey—one filled with brilliance, beauty, blessings, burdens, and beatdowns—as I search for meaning in this question. I am a native son with two homes. This duality of Blackness holds both my rich African ancestry and my American birth—celebrated, copied, misunderstood, envied, caricatured, stereotyped, full of humanity, yet, at times, stripped of it. Too often, Black masculinity is reduced to physical prowess while the spiritual, emotional, and intellectual dimensions of our humanity—our full breath—are ignored. But what does it truly mean to be a Black man?

I feel like the most vulnerable part of me is missing from society's understanding of what it means to be a Black man in America—and the world. I've learned that how you see me says more about who you are than who I am. Too often, others try to define me—who they think I am, who they want me to be. All I've ever wanted—like so many of my Black brothers—is the freedom to simply be. To dream. To love. To stumble, to rise, start again. To make the most of my days and leave behind a legacy that matters—one that makes the world a little bit better. Every day, I walk the line between vulnerability and strength, committing myself to life, to love, and to learning—all in the most beautiful and meaningful way I can.

Cool Fire: A Black Man's Poetic Odyssey came to life as a way for me to speak my truth and share a perspective on what it means to be a Black man in these times. I chose poetry and photography because the fusion of words and images is its own kind of liberation—one that frees me and, hopefully, others who are striving to do the same.

This collection of poems is a journey of discovering my voice—a testament to faith, resilience, and passion. It carries a certain coolness, a commitment to truth, and a deep gratitude for the timeless voices of our ancestors, the pulsing rhythms of our present, and the whispered hopes of our future.

Through these verses, I invite you to step into the intricate dance of identity, desire, spirit, heart, voice, vision, and intellect. Each poem moves toward sparking curiosity, challenging perspectives, and pushing us to question ourselves as we seek to understand our joys, the struggles we endure, the love we cherish, and the dreams we pursue.

Welcome to a journey of reflection, revelation, reimagining, and celebration of humanity—and of what it means to be a Black man. This work is an invitation to a conversation, an exploration of our shared humanity and intimacy, a reimagining of Black masculinity, and a recognition of the legacy that binds us. Let's walk this path together, and may these words resonate with you as deeply as they have with me in writing them.

Love you!
Robert L. Dortch, Jr.

"For God has not given us a spirit of fear, but of power, love, and a sound mind."

— 2 Timothy 1:7

The West African Adrinka symbol "Dwennimmen" represents strength and humility.

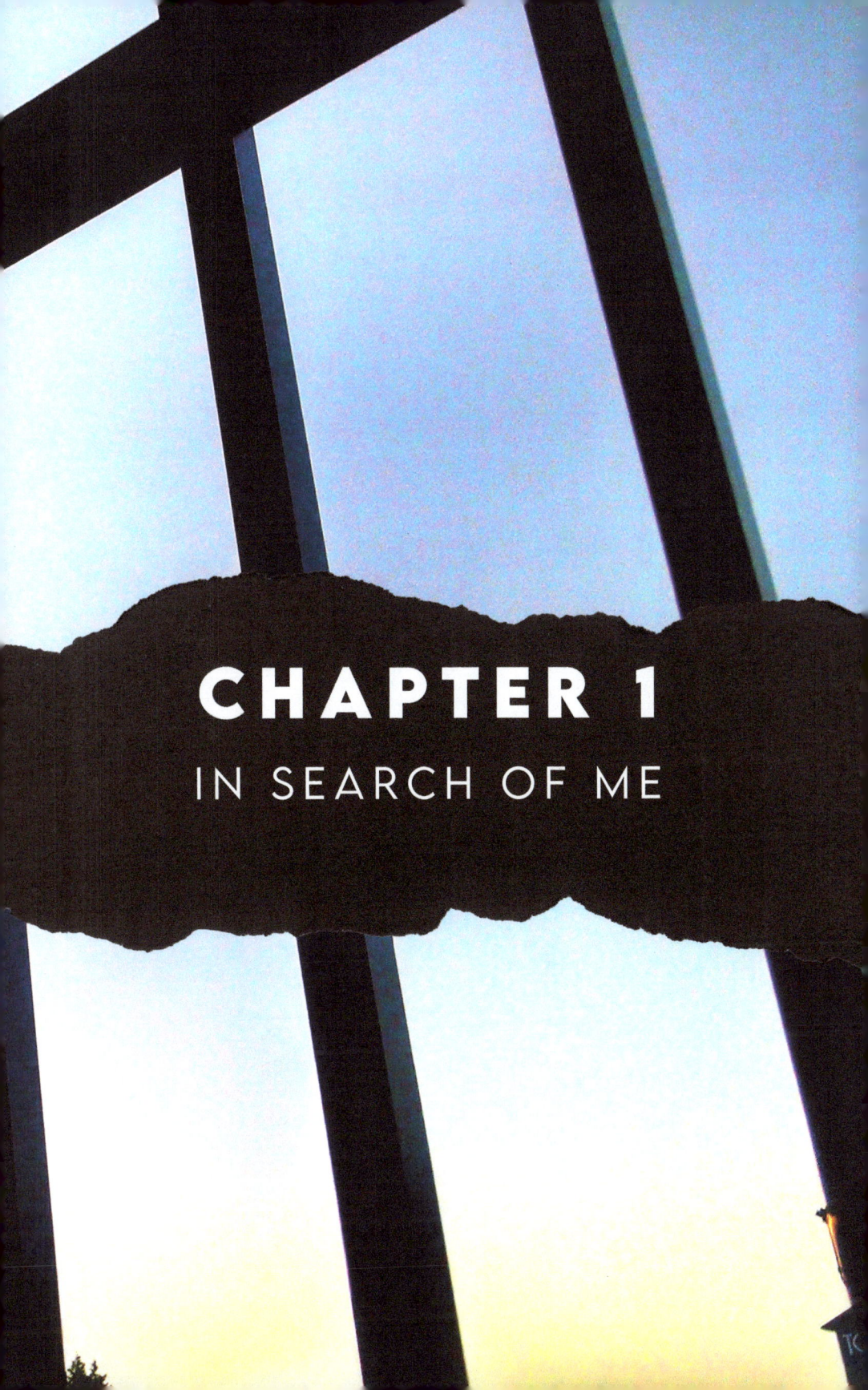

CHAPTER 1
IN SEARCH OF ME

WHEN I HEAR THE VOICE OF
BALDWIN

Like the beating of the drum, I hear your words echoing, lamenting, refusing to be silenced and buried in yesterday, transcending a time that is no more and reaching into now.

The vibration of your utterance awakens me from an already restless night and arouses me as you invite me to come to you and listen. Shsss... as you call me to be more than what I've become.

Yours is a chosen voice, telling the sojourn of the unheard, denied, despised, and deferred, and your words won't let go. They keep coming by sound, by pen, and will not be deterred because our story must be told; we were born to be free, damn what they say.

Sometimes, all I can do is cry when you speak and describe a hell I know so well when I continue to be hunted by a wounded nation who abuses herself every time she seeks to castrate my spirit and terrorize me with her chains, ropes, guns, rapes, laws, and the lies she tells and denies when she speaks of me and my blackness.

Yet every time I hear you, I know I'm closer to being who I was born to be.

Robert L. Dortch, Jr.

Your words are a courageous declaration of your desire for me to say yes to me, my beauty, my humanity, my love, my blackness, and yes to our story. Oh, my beautiful Black child.

The passion of your prophetic demands I do more than bemoan my circumstance.

I AM A BLACK MAN is more than a masculine declaration. It is a revolutionary act of self-acceptance wrapped in love, defiance, divinity, and destiny.

You open up my eyes to a world beyond these borders as you hold up a mirror for us to witness ebony excellence everywhere we are.

Whenever I receive a message from you, it's like a gift from God, reminding me I am a chosen generation, a royal priesthood. I am holy, holy, holy.

Your words are my declaration of liberation, calling me to escape to my freedom, to write, to bear witness, to proclaim, to stand up, to embrace my beauty, my style, my soul, my sensuality, my spirituality, my humanity, and all of me.

...and when I do, then I might just be free.

The Conversation

1. How do Baldwin's words transcend time in this poem?

2. What does the phrase "I AM A BLACK MAN" signify in the context of this piece?

3. How does the poem connect personal identity with broader social struggles?

GETTING TO KNOW ME

Staring in the mirror, asking me,
"What do you see when you see me?"

I see a stranger inside of me

Fighting like hell to break free

Duality inside and out

What's this feeling all about?

What you see is me, but it's not fully me, you see

I'm a brother in the midst of a crisis of identity

So I must go create a space for wellness to dwell

'Cause I really want to be well again, if I ever was

Turning down the noise of am I good enough to be with anyone, especially me

Learning how to be with me is where I must start this chapter if I ever hope to be free

My emancipation and liberation are on the line

As I sigh, I ask God, "Why?"

Another mountain to climb

What will be different this time?

Tired of slipping on internal stones and falling off of emotional cliffs

Healing a heart broken by life and unwise choices

I still hear the cries of aborted voices

I close my eyes and pray

Dreaming that this will be a different day

Why does my heart feel this way?

I weep in my sleep

Why is trauma labeled as a sin?

I wake and start again, again and again

Striving to become my own best friend

Walking in the sunrise, longing to feel the morning sun against my skin

Maybe I need to let go of we and go be with me so I can get to know the stranger inside of me.

The Conversation

1. How does the poem describe the process of reconciling with the "stranger" inside?

2. In what ways does the poem explore the idea of self-acceptance and the path to emotional freedom?

3. What role do spirituality and faith play in the poet's journey toward healing and understanding their identity?

I AM

I am a Black man with the last name Dortch.
I am an American Citizen.
I am a Son.
I am a Father.
I am from Virginia, born and raised in the former
Capital of the Confederacy.
I read. I write. I vote.
I am educated with a couple of degrees.
I inspire people for a living.
I get paid to think.
I have aborted life.
I am a believer in life.
I am a family man.
I am divorced.
I fall sometimes.
I am a leader.
I am a philanthropist.
I am a coach.
I travel.
I have a passport.
I zip-line.
I boogie board.
I hike. I bike. I run.
I've completed three marathons.
I am a baker of cakes and cookies.
I laugh.
I cry.

I care. Once, I freed a bird who was trapped in the
ice on a frigid winter day.
I hurt.
I grieve.
I am a Baptist preacher who believes Jesus, Allah,
Jehovah, and Buddha are related.
I am successful.
I am intelligent and articulate.
I will cuss you out.
I am sapiosexual.
I am complicated.
I love love.
I am more than what you think you see.
I am a beautiful man, and I am not the only one. We are everywhere.
When will you see us?

The Conversation

1. How does the poet's list of personal attributes build a picture of his identity?

2. What impact does the repetition of "I am" have on you as the reader?

3. How does the poet reconcile the complexities of his identity?

HOODS, HOODIES, & HOPE

Why the cool pose, you ask?
Why do we wear the mask?
Do a mental rewind of ivory-colored hoods
Riding in the night picking strange fruit
Yesterday, Emmitt Till for a playful whistle
Trayvon Martin for iced tea and Skittles?
Today, George Floyd you kill for a twenty-dollar bill
And you keep taking our breath away
Yesterday and today still feel like the same day
Can you still hear the sounds of souls marching to overcome?
Through our mothers' and fathers' faith, we believed the price was
paid in full to move us to that post-racial promise land of
gated hoods where you mislabel my hoodie and skin as a
sin worth dying for
I cry for you and me, for our sons, for us, and while I try to love you, I wonder
When will America see the beautiful boys we call sons?
When will our sons see the America you call beautiful?

The Conversation

1. What is the significance of the "hoodie" in this poem?
2. How does the poem use historical references to comment on current events?
3. What emotions does the poem evoke in you regarding identity and safety?

PHARAOH'S LOST CHILD

Sometimes you think you know, but you don't really know until you do and then the world, as you know, changes forever

You ask, "What's this know I'm talking about?"

You tried to erase our clout

Delete our lineage

Yet the secret is out

We've got news to shout about beyond the pews

23andMe took me on a scientific trip

It opened my eyes and helped me see

I am he

Just look at my eclectic family tree

American born

Nigerian and Ghanaian, too

German Dutch that comes from you

Based on the shss you did to my ancestral mommy

It's all in my complicated tapestry

But wait, there's so much more to my story untold

Royal blood traveling through me

Slave I'll never be

No shackles for me

Told you "I always be FREE"

It just can't be 'cause you couldn't see the king in me

And sometimes neither could we

Even when you said that's crazy talk, go sit down somewhere, as I walk that walk

You know that walk and

Talk that talk, you know that talk as I stroll with my head held high

I smile that smile, you know that smile

Now I know, what I know, what I know to be true

Noble child

Son of the Nile

Sit with that for a while

I just smile as I think about that fact

The historical tract

How could that be?

It's all in the genealogy

I AM HE

I AM the one they've been searching for, for quite a while,

I am Pharaoh's lost child.

The Conversation

1. How does this poem use personal genealogy as a metaphor for reclaiming identity and heritage?

2. In what ways does the poem challenge historical erasure and celebrate the resilience of ancestral lineage?

3. How does this poem's tone evolve from questioning to self-assurance, and how does this shift impact you?

CHAPTER 2
WHEN I SPEAK OF INTIMACY

INDEPENDENT LOVE

Like flowing water and timeless nights
Like forever skies and an endless sunrise
So is my love for you
It moves without form, yet it holds your heart and cares for you
You wonder how it could care for others, too?
That twist of independent love confuses tradition,
Therefore, it's looked upon with suspicion
Yet the same love that frees you scares you,
So you decide to let my love go
So you can find a love you know that fits your flow,
So what happens now?
Where does independent love go from here?
I don't know...
I just go.

The Conversation

1. How does the poem challenge traditional notions of love?

2. What does "Independent love" mean to you after reading the poem?

3. How does the poem convey the tension between freedom and tradition in love?

MISFITS LONGING

Why do I long to belong where I can be free to be me?

Is it my head resting on the inside of your thigh?

Is it our palms connected and our fingers intertwined?

Is it inside your heart where my heart is searching for rest and healing from years of aching and breaking?

Is it when our desirous bodies merge into a sensual solace?

Time meets itself when we're together

We fit disproportionately into our destiny

We are an incongruent match that equals one

We belong.

The Conversation
1. How does the poem describe the feeling of longing?
2. In what ways do the misfits "fit" together, according to the poem?
3. How does the imagery of sensual solace contribute to the theme of desire?

PASTORAL EROTIC

Their eyes meet beneath the surface
Her hands touch his, and his lips caress her beauty with words
Their kisses caress and comfort.
Their bodies move like ballet dancers
Infinite talks of love unspoken yet understood
Smiles share stories of struggle and success
Tears that grieve while growing trust
Sacred orgasms
Evening hellos turn into sleepless midnights
Passionate pursuits
Appetites longing for more
She releases her love
He re-imagines love
Invitations to remember a timeless love that began before today
Culinary curiosities that commune
Hugs that hold them and heal past hurts
Their hearts imagine love without walls
Sensual salvation
Love is born again
God is a witness to an intimate worship
When she calls him Baby, he melts into new possibilities of what can be
Her eyes seduce him to stillness
Her lips caress him to calm.

The Conversation

1. How does the poet blend spiritual imagery with physical intimacy to create a sense of "intimate worship?"

2. In what ways does the poem reflect the healing power of love and its ability to transform past hurts into new possibilities?

3. How do the references to "sensual salvation" and "sacred orgasms" challenge traditional ideas of love and spirituality?

WHEN THE STARS SEE LOVE

The night has come, and the stars are witness to their love

As she lay naked under their gaze, they whispered while she waited for him to accept her invitation

His heart racing to meet her love and experience the joy that comes with the beauty of night

Their bodies unite with the celestial beings who gave birth to their love before there was a beginning

She is his Eve

Her spirit has always been

Before there was breath in his being

God meant for her to love him back to wholeness and

For him to heal her with his creative touch

The heavens smiled while it listened to their melodic rhythms travel through the darkness of night and made the angels blush with joy

Yes! This is their time to love.

The Conversation

1. How does the poem use celestial imagery to elevate the intimacy and spirituality of the couple's connection?

2. In what ways does the poem reflect on the idea of predestined love and its role in healing and wholeness?

3. How does the description of love as a union between the earthly and the divine influence the tone and message of the poem?

CHAPTER 3

IN THE SPIRIT

INSIDE THE SILENT MIND

Come, come with me and see
Take a look around
Noise turned down
Imagine a mind without sound
Absent of clicks, ringing, booming beats or hateful frowns
Life slows down
Hope and joy abounds
Come, come with me, and see what you see
Inside you'll find
Stillness lives in the silent mind
Suffering ceases
Anxiety peaces

> Chaos is calm
> Granny told me remember that Psalm
> It says there is a balm for me
> Come, come see where Spirit is free
> No place here for fear to beat on me
> Like water, my thoughts are clear
> Healing happens here
> Breathe and turn the noise down
> Come, come with me and see life slow down
> Tell me what you find
> When you look inside your silent mind?

The Conversation

1. How does the poem describe the process of finding peace and stillness within the "silent mind"?

2. In what ways does the poem connect spiritual wisdom, such as the reference to the Psalm, with the calming of internal chaos?

3. How does the poem invite the reader to envision a state of peace and calm, and what role does imagination play in this process?

A SOUL IN SEARCH OF

My soul aches for a love that hugs my heart,
stories that soothe my scars, and
shines like the sun on Sunday morning.

A love that dances like diamond dreams in the dawn.

A love that longs to lay with me in lavender gardens and
lingers to sip liquid laughter.

A love that moves in the midst with the mist, breathes beauty,
trust truth, kisses kindness, grows from grief and
generates genius when we love and makes magic out of
moody moons that meander into majestic mornings.

My heart sojourns in search of enchanted eyes,
sacred smiles, and sweet smells of your sugar that stays
after our sojourns of peaceful playfulness, sensual songs,
silent shouts and walks around the world together
wishing for wise waterfalls to wash us in wonder and
wash our worries away into memories who've moved beyond us.

My mind pursues purpose, prophetic protest,
justice that is just and creates colorful conversations that
connects your cool with my cool, beats that bless us both and
regal rhythms that reach to the heavens and
hears our holy, holy, holy, holla.

My body stretches for a hand to hold on to,
as we hope for healing when our hearts are broken, and
tears that triumph over tragedy.

Is my soul seeking you?

The Conversation

1. What is the poet searching for in this piece?
2. How does the imagery of nature contribute to the spiritual journey described?
3. What does the poem reveal about the poet's view of love and spirituality?

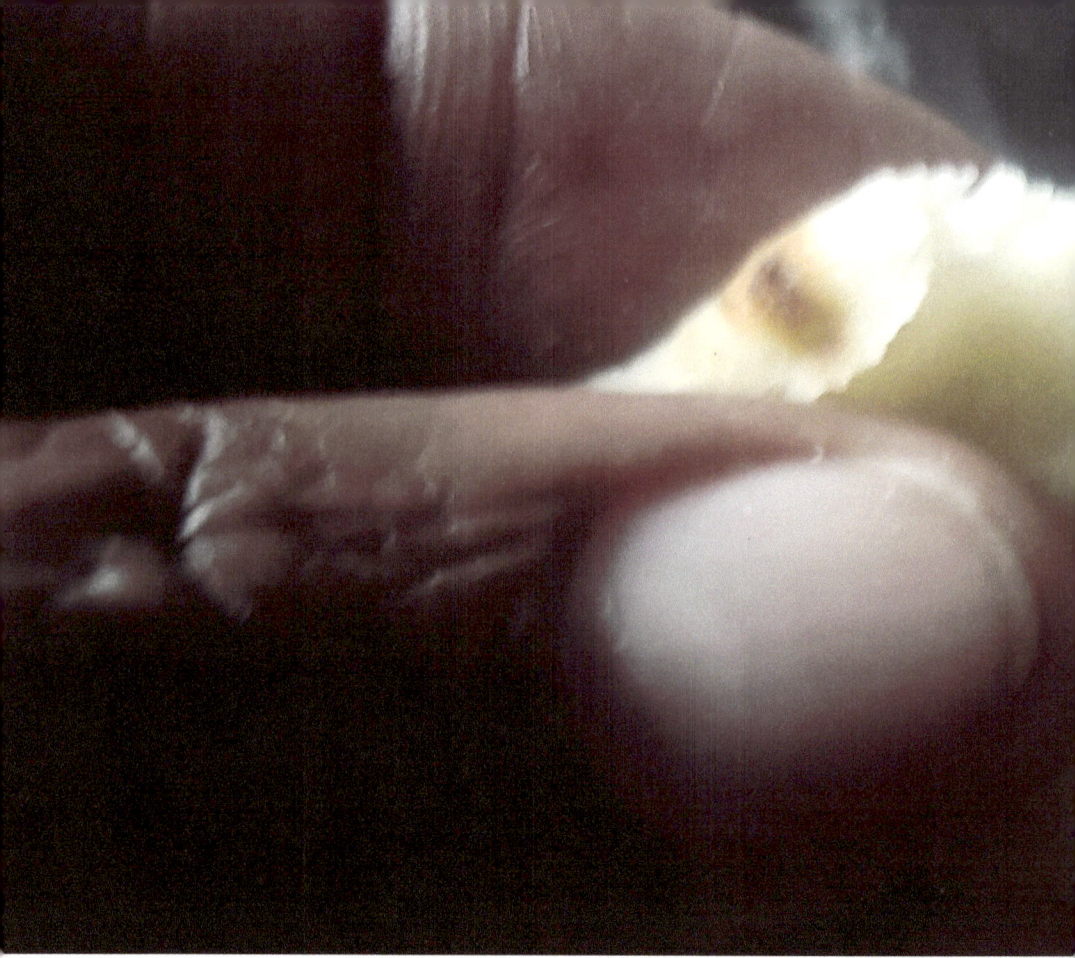

SPIRITUAL TENACITY

How can a spirit grow strong when my body is weak, worn, worried?

How do I pray when my pain reminds me of my reality?

How do I believe when I feel beat down like beats like beats like beats?

My soul is strong that way.

The Conversation

1. How does the poem describe the struggle between body and spirit?

2. What role does faith play in the poet's resilience?

3. How does the poem reflect the poet's inner strength?

MAN'S MYSTERY

Longing for you before I ever knew you could be

You started as an idea in the Divine's imagination

Some call you creation

Many days I come looking for you...

Trying to find you even though I've heard you're already in me

They tell the story of how from you I came and to you I'll return

If we're so close like that... I ask

How can we be strangers?

As I ask for your presence

Searching for your essence

Your arrival was beyond what I could comprehend

As you appeared in the morning dawn as I moved through the garden

As the sun was rising, your crown came into the light

Beauty beyond

Your indigo nights wrap us in darkness

The stars flicker in the night like candlelight

I lie awake inhaling your essence

You linger and move with me even when I don't know you're here

I feel your breath in the wind

I smile as I remember my mornings with you

The blues turn without notice

You shower us

Your heat is your passion

We don't know yet; there will come a day when I won't treat you right

and I'll try to do better

Can I call you baby... or is that too soon for new lovers to be that way?

Why do we call you mother when you feel more like

an ancient lover seducing me back into oneness with you?

You are a river flowing,

You are a cool breeze

You are a mystery to me

I've walked naked with you, feeling your dew on the bottom of my souls as I tried to reconnect with a place that seems so far away from what we used to be

Distant lovers were we?

Did I come from you and will you come for me?

Here I am and I hear you

I want to know can I be free with you?

The Conversation

1. What does the poem seek to understand about existence?

2. How does the poem explore the relationship between humanity and the divine?

3. What emotions does the poem evoke about the mysteries of life?

JUST BEFORE MORNING

While morning still sleeps,
I hear me talking to me

Asking me can I see

I drive in the stillness of night

Where sounds are muted by rest

Yet my mind hasn't got the memo

Roads going to unfamiliar spaces

Spirit races to dangerous places in the mind

Heart pounding sounds like base inside my head.

The Conversation

1. How does the poet use the imagery of driving at night to reflect the inner turmoil of the mind and spirit?

2. In what ways does the contrast between external stillness and internal chaos create tension in the poem?

3. How does the poem explore the relationship between restlessness and self-reflection during the quiet hours before morning?

SILENT JOY

For My Granny

A quiet ride home
Silenced by illness
Quiet stillness
No words are spoken
No sadness here
God gives no fear
I see joy in her eyes
This time in life is our prize
We share a peaceful gaze
Grateful for these final days
Her eyes smile wide
My hand she squeezes
Her stories now told by touch
The memory never fades
Love moves slowly between us
She winks and nods, gold crown shining
A hug goodnight just to let me know
No matter what life will bring
We are going to be alright.

The Conversation

1. How does the poet use silence and stillness to convey the depth of love and connection in this poem?

2. In what ways does the poem highlight the importance of non-verbal communication in moments of shared intimacy and understanding?

3. How does the imagery of "gold crown shining" and "her stories now told by touch" symbolize the enduring legacy of the grandmother's love and wisdom?

A Q&A ABOUT LOVE

Can we just talk about love?
In the beginning, love
Asking for love,
Looking for love
Praying for love
Could it be love?
Will you go with me kind of love?
What kind of love is our kind of love?
A love language
A love song
A love story
A love supreme
An around the way kind of love
A falling in love first love kind of love
A blinded by love all night long kind of love
An I'll be loving you always kind of love
A just me or maybe not kind of love
A lady sings the blues love jones kind of love
An if loving you is wrong kind of love
A staying in and out of my life kind of love
A forever never stay together just for this season kind of love
A let's just kiss and say goodbye kind of love
A love lost
A lost love
A where did love go kind of love?
A broken-hearted kind of love
What happened, Paul?

The Conversation

1. How does the poet explore different stages and types of love in this poem, and what does this variety suggest about the nature of love?

2. What emotional response does the repetition of "kind of love" evoke, and how does it contribute to the poem's overall impact?

3. How does the poem blend cultural references with personal reflections to create a universal exploration of love?

IMPERFECTLY BEAUTIFUL

Imperfect beauty is who you are to me.

And you know what, baby?

That's what makes you fine to me.

You don't seek to disguise your splendor with off-the-rack designs that cover up your spiritual curves.

Your elegance is seen in the richness of a reality that knows what it's like to wake up the day after losing sleep over love.

Flawed love is perfect love because it's real in telling you, "Damn, it ain't easy to love you."

Cynical love is not love but unwillingness to forgive yourself for believing and letting go of a real pain that can expire if you move on.

Never was, is, or will be…

You don't hide behind made-up prettiness painted on with bottles filled with dreams that will never come true.

Your scars turn me on because they reveal your story filled with aching for more than a replay of the past.

I taste the saltiness of your secrets, which reveal your despair of love gone astray.

Imperfect love is a fallen love that exposes the spectacle of happily ever after.

When the spell is broken, you realize that loving and sexing ain't the same, even though sometimes it feels that way.

Your nakedness captures me.

It's seasoned with the patience that demands me to love slow.

I want to savor your wrinkles, caress your silver strands, and just be with you as you age into eternal.

The Conversation

1. How does the poet redefine beauty and love through the lens of imperfection in this poem?

2. In what ways does the poem challenge traditional or idealized notions of love and intimacy, and why is this important?

3. How does the poet use imagery of scars, wrinkles, and aging to highlight the depth of love that grows through life's challenges and imperfections?

MY DEAR FRIEND

For Joel

We first met in a sacred place on a sunny day, surrounded by yellow sunshine—the richness of spring in a city with a past filled with pain and hope.

Remember the garden high on the hill?

We mused about our beginnings, where we'd come from, and how he'd come to this place.

On that day, our words walked us to common ground.

As our talk was about the end,

I asked, "How can I help you in your new role?"

Your reply was, "Can we be friends?"

Your invitation surprised me, and there was a silent pause; we smiled and agreed to start with a walk.

As time moved forward, a friendship began

Over morning talks with coffee and tea in the cafe,

Afternoon walks down by the river,

Talks about manhood, love, our sons, and life,

Mountain bike rides on rolling hills.

That was a stormy day I'll never forget.

In your West Virginia home, I found rest as I prepared for one of my greatest test.

I remember the call—the words you shared: an unwelcome stranger had entered your mind, and you didn't know what tomorrow would bring, or how much time was left to share.

On our last walk together, you spoke about friendship and gratitude. You explained the type of golden leaves that were flying from the trees, and that we didn't know how much time remained—that this might be our last time.

Friends we did become.

Friends, we will always be.

This is not the end,

so goodbye for now, until we meet again,

My friend.

The Conversation

1. How does the poet use vivid imagery of nature and shared activities to illustrate the depth and progression of the friendship?

2. In what ways does the poem explore the concept of time and its impact on relationships, particularly in the face of uncertainty and loss?

3. How does the poet convey both the finality of parting and the enduring nature of the friendship, creating a balance between grief and hope?

NIGHT VISITS

She shows up unannounced in my dreams when the day has slowed down

A pleasant late-night surprise before sunrise

She knocks on my mind, inviting herself into my space

She blends with my being provoking sensual scenes

Without warning, she moves to my heart and...

....immediately hooks up with the rhythms and flows of my beats

Her presence is easygoing and causes erotic curiosity

Her fingers massage my mood, creating a restless and smoldering passion

There is silence

Where did she go?

Then there is no night

Morning comes

Her fragrance lingers long after she says goodbye

Her melodious moans replay again and again inside my soul

I wonder, is this what happens when a feminine power comes into a masculine heart?

The Conversation

1. How does the poet use the imagery of night to convey feelings of love?
2. What does the presence of the woman in the poet's dreams symbolize?
3. How does the poem explore the connection between dreams and reality?

STRANGERS OVERNIGHT

Loved erased by pain

What was is no more

Hidden hurt attempts to delete the sacred and sublime

From something to nothing overnight

There are no words

Empty spaces silent with memories of what we used to be

Was this an imaginary reality of a love I hoped would be?

Eternal no more

Grief may catch up before I move on to the next chapter of love, but for now, I'm too numb to feel the pain that comes from breakup...

Is this self-inflicted conflict born from prideful souls who will never admit that what we had was good when it was right?

Is there compassion for suffering souls who fumble in and out of love?

Is this soon to be forgotten because it may be too painful to remember how good it was when it was good?

My heart has retreated from you and from what we once were because trust is no more

Broken bonds that were not strong enough to weather surprise storms

Caught off guard by the overnight demise of a love we imagined was eternal but was just an extended one-night stand created by hurt people who continue to hurt people so we exit this love without saying goodbye, and we leave knowing that what we had was good while it lasted but today you became a stranger overnight, and my heart has now gone back inside to heal from the hurt caused by loving you.

Goodnight.

The Conversation

1. How does the poet describe the transition from connection to estrangement, and what emotions does this evoke?

2. In what ways does the poem reflect on the complexities of trust and the fragility of relationships?

3. How does the imagery of "empty spaces" and "broken bonds" contribute to the poem's exploration of loss and healing?

I WISH YOU

LOVED me

WHEN LOVE EXPIRES

The distance grows

Time moves

The heartaches and breaks because we look into tomorrow and there is no you and there is no us

The heart grows faint... as we walk away in opposite directions, looking to escape the pain of a love that has expired.

The fight is ending

Who wins?

"I need time for me" are the famous words of love gone missing

There is no good morning love

Midday love

The nights are absent of you

Should I fast from you for lent?

Someone asks about where you went.

I respond, "Away from me."

I look for you throughout the day only to find that you are neither thinking nor looking for me

You show up nowhere

Like a ghost, you are gone, baby, gone.

The Conversation

1. How does the poet use time as a metaphor for the gradual dissolution of love?

2. In what ways does the poem explore the tension between grief and acceptance in the aftermath of a relationship?

3. How does the imagery of absence and distance highlight the emotional impact of love's end?

CHAPTER 5
CAN YOU HEAR ME

WHEN WILL TOMORROW COME

for Langston Hughes

While I, too, sing America, I weep because tomorrow is taking too damn long to come...

So what should we do until tomorrow comes?

My granny once told me to believe what the Bible says, that weeping may endure for a night, but joy comes in the morning.

I always wanted to know why we always waiting for joy and if joy can sometimes come before tomorrow because my nights are long, my head hurts, and my heart aches for a tomorrow that's taking a long time to come.

When yesterday's prejudice keeps returning and won't go away, I find myself asking, "When will tomorrow come?"

Do I stand, and where do I place my hand when America sings, "My country 'tis of thee sweet land of liberty?" Yet liberty's words turn sour, and America the Beautiful has no makeup to cover up the ugliness of its inhumanity to citizens who suffer in silence; I can take a knee until tomorrow comes.

While you gerrymander the lines of my neighborhood in search of votes to bring back the political ghost of an alabaster past, I will keep voting until tomorrow comes.

When the Commonwealth creates uncommon wealth for some while other brothers and sisters starve to live, I will save, invest, and build my wealth until tomorrow comes.

When injustice rises from the dead and rears its racist past, I find myself wondering again, when will tomorrow come?

When men in judicial robes decide to roll back the clock on what a woman can do with the life inside her being, I will fight for her until tomorrow comes.

When my child asks me, "Daddy, how long will they hate me because I'm Black like the night?" I find myself saying, "Son, I really don't know when tomorrow will come."

When courts decide to resurrect laws buried deep down in the annals of our past to shut down the doors of learning to America's young, gifted, and Black, I will read, write, learn, and create until tomorrow comes.

When blood trickles down liberty's cheek, bullets from guns blast our children's dreams away, and votes can't be found to say "no more," I will keep praying for tomorrow to come.

When life, liberty, and the pursuit of happiness become just another line quoted like a nursery rhyme while Black like me, still can't breathe, I will fight, I will unite, I will dissent, I will vote and build my own table until tomorrow comes.

The Conversation

1. How does the poet address the ongoing struggle for justice in this poem?

2. What emotions does the poet evoke through the use of rhetorical questions?

3. How does the poem reflect the poet's frustration and hope?

A MOMENT IN HARLEM

As wings landed, heart racing, anticipation because I couldn't wait to see her

As the driver crossed onto125th

There she was waiting and swaying in winter's setting sun

She hugs me with fist-bump greetings and head nods

Her name is Harlem

Heart opened wide

Soul naked with truth

Energy flowing like water falling in love with the fresh breath of morning

Her people miss no beats

While they create heat to keep life warm

Her children dance to their own rhythm

Just walk the streets on a chilly winter night, and you'll see my muse has many moods

Spiritual moans and gospel cries

Jazzy blues

Rhymes and beatboxing beats

Symphony of life unfolding

Harlem hustles for a living

She winks back at you when she recognizes you trying to fit into her flow

You don't know love until she welcomes you with a morning sunrise

She's Black Mecca rooted in life, love and where liberation lives

She makes room for revolution to happen here

We remember so well the Theresa Hotel

Remember the lives lost because she knows freedom comes at a cost

So don't sleep and romanticize Harlem's love

While her life is wrapped in prose and song to soothe us, her pain lingers

Blessings bestowed by those who came before, some names we know like Angelou, Baldwin, Dubois, Hughes, Malcolm, Thurghood, Powell, Pac, and Zora, and there are so many more who we may never know, yet in their footsteps we walk and on their shoulders we stand

Harlem love is real love wrapped in something I can feel but cannot explain

As I sat on the plane lingering in my moments with Harlem

I heard a voice say

Where are you coming from classy man?

I smiled and said, "Harlem," and she said, "I understand."

The Conversation

1. How does the poet personify Harlem, and what does this reveal about its essence and significance?

2. In what ways does the poem blend historical reverence with the present-day experience of Harlem?

3. How does the poem use sensory details—sight, sound, and movement—to immerse you in the streets of Harlem?

MANIFESTATION

We are they

Manifestation of prayers elders pray for us every day

We are they

Born of ancestors who found a way to live despite injustice in their way

We are they

Who have been told the stories of yesterday that show us the way

We are they

America's prey who got away

and know freedom is our only way forward

Yes, there is a cost we pay

Don't buy what they say

We were born to be this way

While there is a delay,

We see the way

We manifest free today.

The Conversation

1. How does the poem connect the struggles of ancestors with the present-day fight for freedom in this poem?

2. What does the phrase "We are they" signify about the collective identity of the poet and their community?

3. How does the poem explore the theme of liberation despite the obstacles and delays encountered along the way?

TIKI TORCHES & THE TALENTED 10TH

While the two may never meet as they walk the same street

Prejudiced nationalists are blowing out their torches, going underground, and taking elected seats

While Black elites have to decide again whether to fight back or retreat and go underground to plan their next feat

So history itself repeats.

The Conversation

1. How does the poem compare and contrast the actions of prejudiced nationalists with the Black elite?

2. What does the poem suggest about the cycles of history and the roles people play in perpetuating or challenging them?

3. How does the poem use imagery of "blowing out torches" and "silent retreat" to evoke a sense of urgency in responding to contemporary struggles for justice?

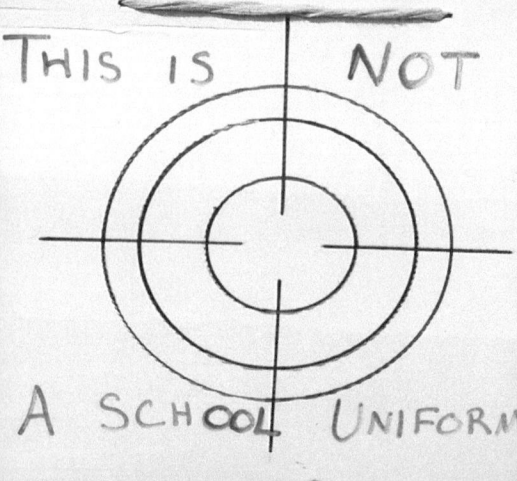

AMERICAN PREY

We live abbreviated lives

Where are we safe?

You call us predators but treat us like prey

Look at the record and what does it say?

We pledge allegiance to

My country 'tis of thee

Where is your love for our babies, Black like me?

Where are we safe?

Who prays for the prey shot down on the playground today?

Who protects the prey?

Who loves the prey who is dying as I write these words today?

Who has been more patriotic than we?

We built the country and fought for us free

We fought for the freedom

But who has benefited less than patriotic prey?

We fight you and we fight for we

Yet you just can't let the brothers be

And go and experience liberty.

The Conversation

1. How does the poet juxtapose patriotism and racial violence?
2. What emotions does the poet evoke by describing being treated as prey?
3. How does the poem call for a reevaluation of American values?

LIFE. BREATH. DEATH IN 8:46

For George

As we cry, "I can't breathe," the world watches us die with cameras rolling like our lives are a reality show and the director will shout, "Cut!"

We ask, "Why?"

How can we stand by and just watch another Black man die?

Have you ever looked in the eyes of a Black man?

Have you seen our hearts smile?

Have you ever felt our love?

How long will you prey on us, but treat us like predators?

When we kneel in peace, you cry foul.

You kneel on our necks with your hands in your pockets, as life leaves our bodies, like this is just another day, while we plead for our lives,

We cry as our breath distances itself from our bodies.

Time stands still while the clock keeps ticking and we close our eyes because we get tired of fighting all the time and we wonder if God's words are true…

Will you be with us always until the end of time or until time ends?

We keep searching for answers to unanswered prayers

If I stop believing in life, then what?

I look in verses to see if I can find peace amid this pain because I'm not okay that for 400 plus years where Black lives don't seem to matter to anyone but our mothers, children and lovers.

"But Jesus said, 'Somebody touched me for I perceived power going out from me,'" Luke 8:46.

"Which of you convicts me of sin? And if I tell you the truth, why do you not believe me?" John 8:46.

"Mama, I can't breathe."

I can't breathe.

"I can't breathe," were George's last words.

When will you listen? When will you hear us? When will you believe us?

The streets now speak for me and for those who rest in an uneasy peace.

The Conversation

1. How does the poet capture the gravity of George Floyd's death?
2. What role does faith play in the poet's response to racial violence?
3. How does the poem challenge you to reflect on social justice issues?

AM I NEXT?
ACK LIVES MATTER

AGAIN

For Ahmad

When did it start?

When did it begin?

The ruthless attacks on the lives of Black men

Again and again...

Again and again...

DAMN!

Just like infinity, it feels like it has no end...

The ruthless attacks on the lives of Black men

When will it change?

When will it stop?

When will it end?

Or will it just keep happening again and again?

The Conversation

1. How does the repetition of "Again and Again" emphasize the ongoing cycle of violence and injustice Black men face?

2. In what ways does the poem evoke both anger and despair, and how does this duality shape your emotional response?

3. How does the use of rhetorical questions challenge you to confront the persistence of systemic racism and violence?

GRIOTS

Where do our stories live?

Human tomes

The grave whispers, "Come, my child,

Can tell you something?"

Stories speak today about yesterday

Pass it on

We must be told

Human libraries

Wisdom speaking

The heavens weep because you just don't know how much we've done and from where we come

Knowledge abound and unbound

Verbal warriors are we

We expound, genius not written down

Words interwoven like threads of hope, encouraging us to remember we create from where we come

Pass it on

You are the children of those who chose to survive

Will you choose to carry on the work we started?

Future seeking

Stories not forgotten

Can you hear them calling us?

Gather around...

In villages, we speak

Street corners we wrap and commiserate our fate

Barbershops and beauty salons we debate

Pulpit and bars we liberate and libate

They gather to tell our stories, to make us laugh, to help us remember

They debate, they discuss, they inform and inspire

We conspire

Listen...

Stolen legacy

Forgotten knowledge

Wisdom survives

Walking tomes

Pass it on

Tradition lives

Ancient tales

Wisdom survives

Where do our stories live?

Pass it on

Pay attention, my son,

Grown folks are talking.

The Conversation

1. How does the poem emphasize the importance of oral tradition and the role of griots in preserving history and wisdom?

2. In what ways does the poem reflect the interconnectedness between past, present, and future generations?

3. How does the imagery of "walking tomes" and "verbal warriors" contribute to the poem's portrayal of knowledge as a living, evolving force?

Mother Emanuel Way
Memorial District

WE STILL BELIEVE

Our hearts, again, broken by promises not kept,

While our salty tears cry throughout the night

And though we build this nation for free,

we are exiled to live like a garden castaway and find ourselves asking,

"Why does America treat us this way?"

When our hearts are heavy with despair

When the pain sometimes seems too much to bear

When the world doesn't show us love or care

And while we ask, "If this dream of democracy is beyond repair,"

We still believe

When political will goes against us

And we don't know if in God we can trust

We still believe

When the waves of injustice fly high and

laws are passed to bury our hopes and drown our dreams

When defeat appears to be our fate

And democracy shows up late, if at all

When God seems like an unknown variable, at best, and justice closes her eyes for an extended rest

The well of justice has run dry, we ask, "Will it ever flow like a mighty stream?"

We still believe

When hate is worn like a badge of honor and my place of birth celebrates with a recycled vote of four more years of this

When sadness surrounds us in grief and wherever we turn there is no relief

When nationalism is resurrected one more time to repeat outdated lines of racial prejudice against us

We still believe

Hear me when I say

No matter what may come my way on any given day

There's only one way and I tell my sons, "Repeat after me and say:

We must rise again and not succumb to this."

We still believe.

The Conversation

1. How does the poet use repetition of "We still believe" to emphasize resilience and collective strength?
2. In what ways does the poem critique societal and political failures while affirming faith in the possibility of change?
3. How does the poet's tone shift between lamentation and determination, and what effect does this have on the reader?

CAN I LET YOU IN?

Catching it on the outside

Wondering who's on my side

Can I come in and open up to you?

My heart aches from the trauma of this pain

From generation to generation we up against a world who loves then hates the essence of our presence

I fight every day and don't want to fight you.

Where can I go?

What can I do?

Where does peace live?

Am I safe with you?

Am I safe with me?

Are we safe with we?

Where can my heart heal from the stress of this madness?

Is this a test?

All I want to do is lay my head down in a safe place where I can find rest.

The Conversation

1. How does the poet use questions to convey vulnerability and the search for safety and trust?

2. In what ways does the poem address generational trauma and its impact on personal relationships?

3. How does the poet explore the tension between external societal pressures and the need for internal healing and peace?

CHAPTER 6
MY DREAMS

SACRED SHOWERS

The water flows and beautiful streams drop like raindrops from the heavens on her caramel-draped skin

The water sounds like drums caressing her body to dance

Water is her aphrodisiac

Her and the water are natural lovers

Why? What is it about this chemical construct of hydrogen and oxygen that sources her and fuels her so?

Is it to celebrate her birth into a new day?

Could it be to cleanse the saltiness of past sins of heartbreak away?

I watch my caramel mermaid dance with another lover

Why am I confused with a mix of arousal and jealousy of this mysterious relationship?

Can she ever love me this much?

I wonder as my gaze stays fixed on her

She sees me

Her eyes, her body, and her kisses invite me to join her and her longtime lover

This virginal odyssey is new to me...

Her touch welcomes me into this ménage à trois world of timeless passion and timeless pleasure

I pause

Her words soothe me to trust her

I believe her soft utterances as my body adjusts to the liquid heat

The coolness of her breath is her gift to me

My senses start running to join the steam, the sounds, the showers as they dance together

Tonight, she baptizes me

Our bodies connect and commune with the water, with each other…

Her sacred waters flow as an offering of her love for what we are becoming

This is holy. This is God. This is us.

Her aquatic love liberates me

Our love grows

Our bodies glisten as together we smile and say, "Amen."

The Conversation

1. How does the poet use water as a metaphor in this poem?
2. What does the relationship between the woman and water symbolize?
3. How does the poem explore themes of purification and renewal?

MAKE TIME FOR MORNINGS LIKE THIS

This morning, when I rose, I knew there was a gift awaiting my arrival

The sun was already smiling at me and I smiled back with gratitude

The air was fresh so I could breathe the beauty of newness and let go of yesterday, because it is finished.

Today is today

No words need to be spoken between us

we've been here before yet not enough

This silence a gift

Our solitude an unexpected blessing I didn't know I needed until you showed up with today

Life has given us more time to be with me and with us, with this bird humming in the background, creating moods to encourage us to stay here a little while before we turn on what will come later

What we make with this time is up to us

Will I enjoy it or waste it? Will I run with it or away from it?

What will it become is up to me and

Make time for more mornings like this and

give back to the day all that has already come my way.

The Conversation

1. How does the poet describe the significance of a new day?
2. What emotions are evoked by the poet's depiction of morning?
3. How does the poem encourage readers to appreciate the present?

THEY WILL WANT TO KNOW

When our time comes

The elders and ancestors will want to know

What did you do?

Did you get some spirit stuff done?

Did you fight for us to be free?

Did you stand for the children?

Did you remember me?

Did you speak for justice?

Did you believe?

Did you carry on?

And by the way, did you pray?

They will want to know.

The Conversation

1. What responsibilities does the poet feel towards his ancestors?

2. How does the poem connect personal actions with historical legacy?

3. What questions does the poem raise about accountability and legacy?

NOT JUST ANOTHER MORNING

As the door opens,
A rising sun kisses my face
Morning dew rises, creating a sacred space
Good morning to this new day dawning
Trees sway and the breeze makes me smile
The air moods me to stay with her for a while
Dog-walking masked strangers wave "Hi"
Birds ascend in skies blue with smoky clouds nearby
Silence comes for a second
I'm home alone, but I'm not alone
Nonstop calls zooming into my peace
This is a serene yet dangerous scene
For God's sake, don't mistake and forget we're in a pandemic state
Daily updates to remind us of our potential fate
Is an invisible death lurking nearby?
This crisis is real
Can't put into words this mood I feel
Will peace be still?
I'm so confused and yet amused by the breaking news
Will there be protests from virtual pews?
Are we open for business and closed for blessings?
Will history call this a magnificent moment or a murderous one?
Yet I still can see the sun
What kind of day will this be?
Just look up at the sky
What do you see?

The Conversation

1. How does the poem use the imagery of morning and nature to contrast with the reality of living through a crisis?

2. What emotions does the poem evoke regarding the balance between finding peace and facing uncertainty?

3. How does the poem challenge the reader to reflect on the current moment in history and what they "see" in their own lives during times of upheaval?

LIFE

Ending happily ever after never happens to those who wait for miracles

Miracles start before they ever live in a womb just before yesterday was born

I go seeking solace inside of me that's searching for a love to love me back to life

Amid sleepless nights of a meandering mind that travels beyond the night to a place where words start as thoughts beyond the stars

Seeking to know the story of the you I knew before the you you've become

Do we love because we don't know what else to do but hold each other until a better day comes?

Or is this some twisted destiny looking for freedom in the wilderness of a distant intimacy imagined so we walk to this place where time sits and waits because purpose is late

So we look at each other and wonder, Will it show up?

Have we missed it while we were looking for something to distract us from that feeling of what am I suppose to be doing with this life?

So I write today but maybe not tomorrow

Have I missed what I think is late but has already come and gone and found somewhere else to live its dreams because we were too busy wondering what does life really mean?

The Conversation

1. How does the poet use the imagery of time and space to explore the tension between purpose and uncertainty in life?

2. In what ways does the poem challenge traditional notions of love and intimacy, framing them as part of a larger existential journey?

3. How does the poet's reflection on missed opportunities and distractions prompt the reader to consider their own approach to finding meaning in life?

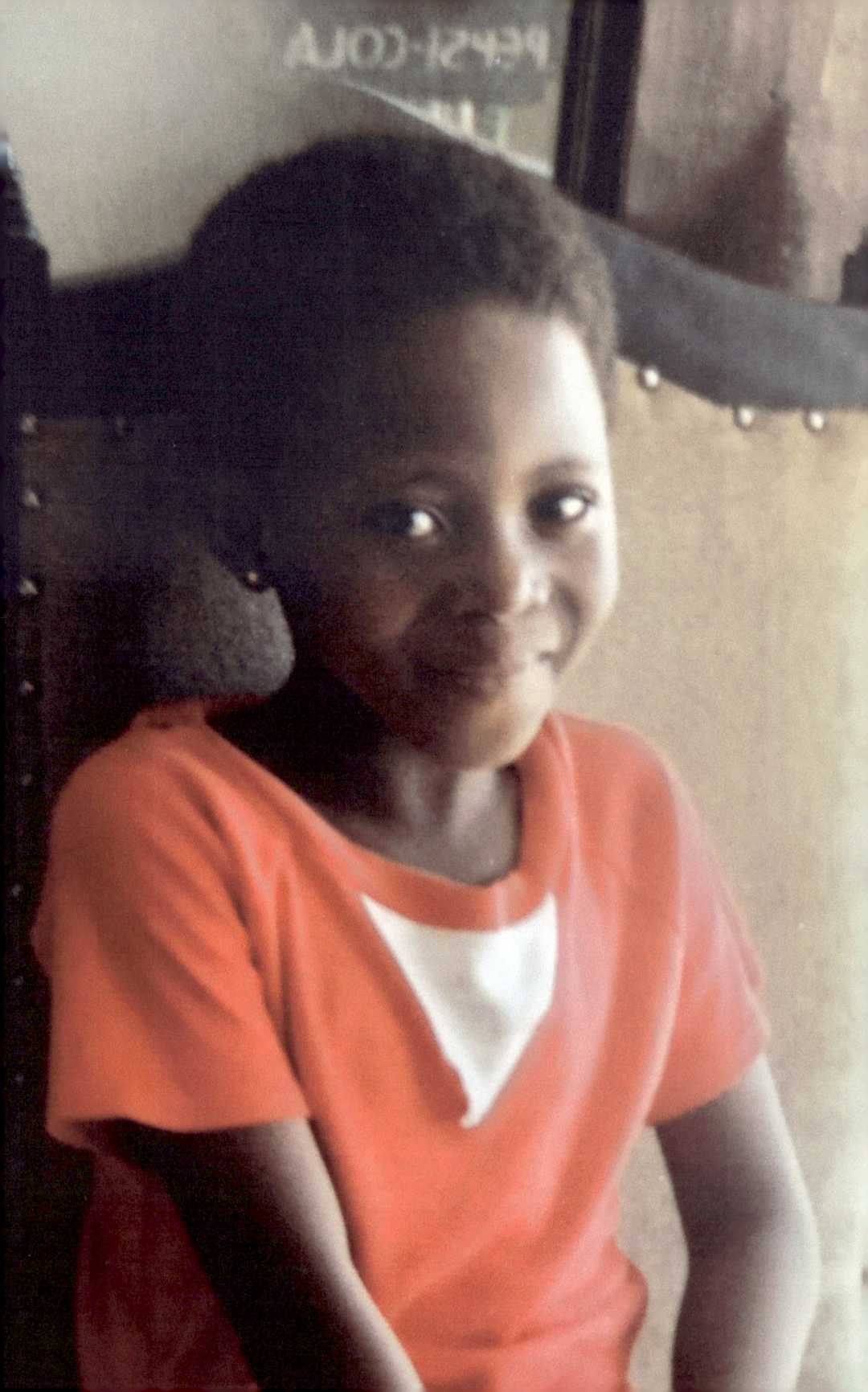

QUEEN BECOMING

Morning, little girl
It started this day
A breath taken
A flower born
Your journey began
A queen becoming
Beauty emerges
Faith in action
Fighting for love
You bounce back again and again
You are destined to win
You make life happen
You are joy
We bow
We smile
We love what you mean to the world and life
Little girl growing up and one day a woman you will become
And now your adventure continues
The future is waiting to meet you in your growing genius to be in the world
We celebrate you and your youness.

The Conversation

1. How does the poet use nature and time as metaphors for a girl's transformation into a woman?
2. In what ways does the poem affirm and uplift the journey of self-love and self-realization?
3. How does the poem's structure reflect the gradual unfolding of identity and empowerment?

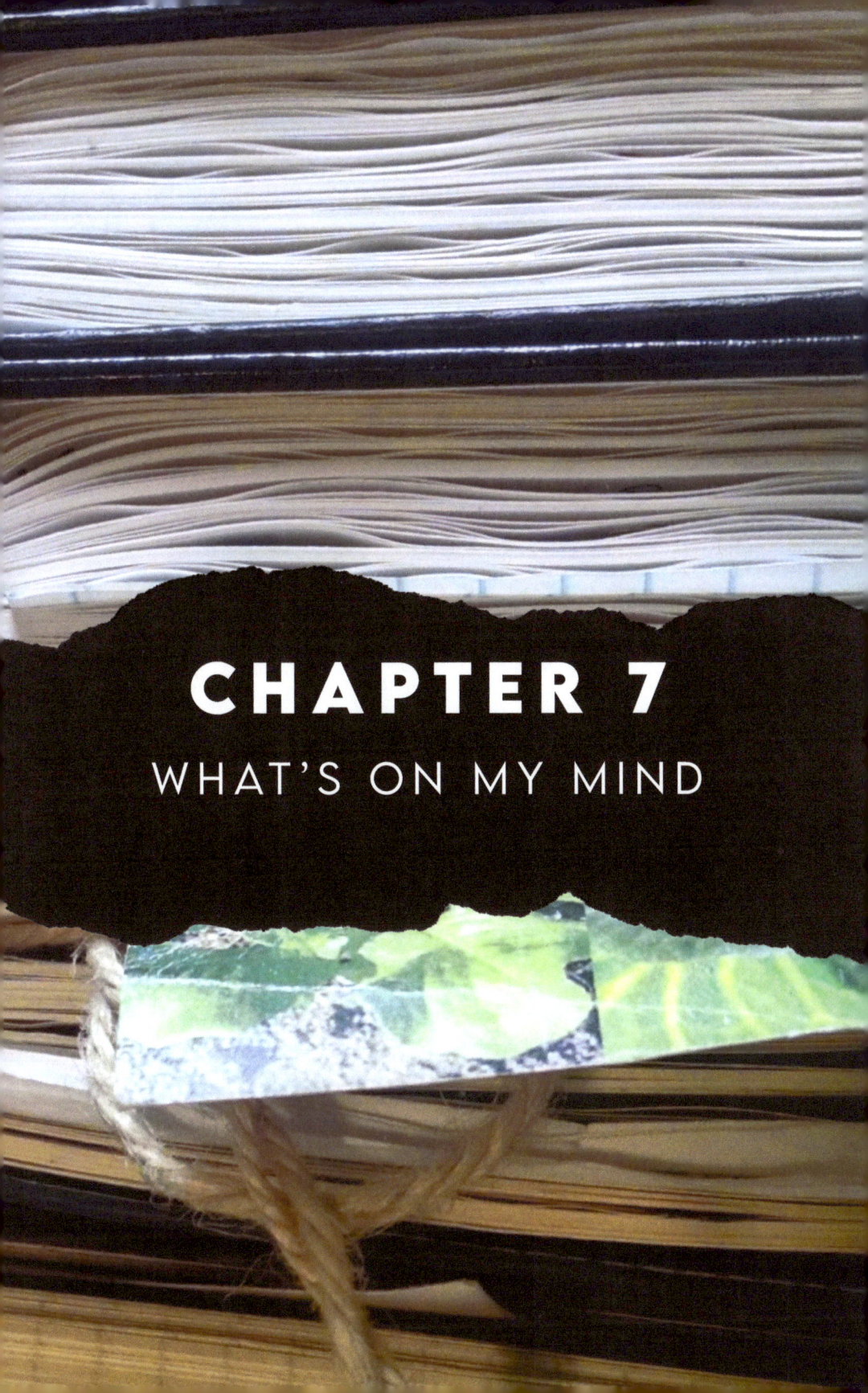

CHAPTER 7
WHAT'S ON MY MIND

BECOMING LIKE YOU

How does a boy learn to be a be a man?

My father taught me in ways I didn't initially understand

It started when I was a son in ways I didn't see until it had already begun

My first memory of you is sitting quietly in your thoughts on the edge of your bed, tying work boots as I jumped around on new legs figuring out the joys of new life with no cares of this world

Through the years, I recall going to baseball games on Sundays in the park with you, as you played hardball.

Every day like clockwork you prepared your work uniform with precision, shining work boots and prepping that brown bag lunch with a Little Debbie cake, a banana and a sandwich for the two jobs you worked.

At 6am your day would start and not until after midnight would it end

I remember looking across the hall into you room and seeing you on your knees praying

Without missing a beat, our lunch money for school would be there on the hi-fi set, shiny coins for my brothers and me

Your love for sports was passed on with you teaching me how to throw a football and catch a baseball with Uncle Moe's glove because I was left-handed like him

You made a wooden backboard and put a hoop with no net in the backyard at 1800 Edwards Ave. so we could play and we turned your beautiful cut green grass into a sandlot for pick up and run and a never a word did you say

On your only day off, you would race us in your boots at Byrd Park, and after you would give us garbage bags to collect aluminum cans so we could have some money in our pockets

When windows we would break and fall through your newly installed storm door you would sit across from us to help us understand why this discipline was a part of the plan

Remember the movies you would take us to see Grease and Bingo Long Traveling All Stars and the Motor Kings

You would surprise us when we go through drive thru to get burgers and fries and you would get your favorite, a vanilla shake and we got to get chocolate

You were our first job recruiter, by walking me up to Bradley's Department store to make sure we had a piece of a job because we had to work

I'll never forget the night you called and said son I'm done if you're going to finish that school it's all on you and yet it was you on that fateful night who came to my rescue at JMU

Looking back I now see your pride in pictures as you stand with a smile

Your first 10k I'll never forget and hearing your voice in the Forest Hill Ave crowd then seeing you smile and wave cheering me on at the halfway point of my first marathon

Fast forward, older you've become and you may not remember many of these moments, but I always will

Just the other day after walking to the store like you often do, I heard my son say, daddy you are becoming just like grandaddy and I thought about that for a while and it made me smile

And I knew that I could be a good man too, just like you.

The Conversation

1. How does the poet use everyday memories and small details to highlight the impact of a father's influence?

2. In what ways does the poem explore the theme of identity and how we unconsciously carry the traits of those who raised us?

3. How does the poem evolve from childhood admiration to adult reflection, and what emotions does this progression evoke?

GIFT OF KNOWING

For Eve

Before time was, knowing was

The essence of life, family, community, and us is built around the gift of knowing

To know you is a spiritual odyssey.

Our intimacy is filled with spirit, emotion, holding, caring, being, and genius

To know is to be secure and supportive in our love.

We're sexual, sensual, and spiritual

We're universal, yet unique...

I ache to touch, to hear, to hold, to see and be seen, to love and be loved, to know

We know what it means to love without words... I see you, Baby.

The touch of your aroused nipples and the warmth from the beads of water dancing on your caramel-complexioned skin compels me to wrap my arms around you

Why so much joy, as my heart aches, as we contemplate an uncertain future?

Is this balance of love about to be debited because of an uncertain future filled with painful goodbyes?

I cry because your beautiful body, as I know it, may never be the same

So I capture you today and us now, but I know I can't hold onto today because I must let go of now and be ready to love you tomorrow, where your beauty will still be

Yet I wouldn't trade the gift of now, of today, and what it means to hear your laugh, to see your smile, to feel your warm body next to mine

Our together is a lifeline about redemption and another chance to love after loss

What does tomorrow hold for us?

Whatever it is... I'll strive to love you the best that I can

I am afraid of our tomorrow, but I play strong because you need my strength

Will our life ever be the same?

The horizon waits to meet us

Will sterile moments and sounds invade our love?

Will our dreams be interrupted and disrupted by doctor visits, procedures, and hospital beds? Or is our future filled with healing moments of miracles of what God can do?

As you lay peacefully asleep, I wonder...

I sit in darkness and dream and cry and hope and pray and believe that there are more mornings like this, where we dance without worry and we sing love songs off-key and we linger in midnight baths, sipping champagne and laughing into a passionate embrace that lulls us to sleep.

What happens now? I wonder...

I keep writing, looking for an answer, a sign of affirmation, something—yes something, so I capture these moments of our love story where knowing is a gift that is always there for us.

The Conversation

1. How does the poem describe the intimacy of knowing someone deeply?
2. What emotions are conveyed through the poem's reflections on love and knowledge?
3. How does the poem blend sensual and spiritual elements?

WHEN BROTHERS CRY

Brother, I cried as I saw your tears fall like rain
Who hears our pain?
The silent suffering seen in tears
Lingering moans for years and years
Longing for a love that feels beyond our reach
Who will teach us to teach our sons how to cry?
How do we call on a God who seems so far away?
The same God who, in the beginning, sent Eve and Adam away?
Can someone see all we go through from day to day?
Believing we deserve hugs to love our pain away
While I stand tall
Who will catch me when I fall?
Like a mighty tree that protects the babies with shade
Who protects me while into the night I fade?
So I cry because I don't know
While I sit here and reflect
I ache from years of emotional neglect
I can't wait any longer for your love to come for me
So I cry in my hope to be free.

The Conversation

1. How does the poem address the emotional struggles of Black men?

2. What does the poem suggest about the need for emotional support and vulnerability?

3. How does the poem challenge traditional notions of masculinity?

FALLING IN LOVE WITH YOU

Where do you start a story that has no beginning nor an end?

When did my falling in love with you begin?

Was it when God said, "Let there be," and there you were?

Let me talk specifically when my falling in love with you began

Was it when you said, "Yes" to carrying me inside your womb for nine months and gave me life?

Was it when you would read and rock me to sleep and sing lullabies and tell me stories of what I could be and who I could become?

Or was it when you said, "Be grateful each and every day," and you taught me how to put my hands together and pray, "God is great and God is good, And we thank Him for our food; By His hand, we must be fed, Give us Lord, our daily bread?"

Or was it when you took my hand and walked me to class on the first day and said, "Remember where you come from; remember who you are, and you can be anything you want to be and remember Mommy loves you?"

Or was it when I wrote you that first love letter and asked, "Will you go with me: yes or no?" and you said, "Yes," and that was still one of the best days of my life until you said, "I don't want to go with you no more?"

Or was it when we had our first dance and I couldn't quite find the beat, but you smiled and forgave me for my two left feet? And as we fast forward, it was you who believed me to a college degree because you could see things in me that I never could see

Because of you, I've been able to go places I never thought I would go, and climb mountains I never thought I could climb, all because you believed in me

Or was it that day when you fell in my arms and you looked at my eyes and you said, "I have less than ninety days to live because I have given all that I can give, but all I want you to remember is the lessons I taught you along the way and, Grandson, everything is going to be okay?"

Or was it when we decided to say, "I do; to have and to hold from this day forward," and committed to raising a family together and, baby, we tried and while the marriage didn't last the love still endures?

While I stand here and talk about how you have loved me, I
Know today that you're more than a mommy and a granny
You're more than a nanny and an auntie, an assistant and a friend
You are so much more
You are the architects of humanity
You are actors, artists, authors, activists, and advocates
You are builders of dreams
You are engineers and entrepreneurs
You are CEOs, designers
You are soldiers
You are musicians
You are ministers
You are pilots, prophets, poets, photographers
You are writers,
You are so much more
So on this day, I would like to say,
You are a queen who doesn't need a crown or throne to lead
You are light, love, and liberation
You are Freedom Fighters
You are power
You are presence

You are purpose
And on this day,
I want to say, "Thank you, thank you."
I come on this day
To salute you
To celebrate you
To honor you
To say, "I love you" and to pray that just as you have loved us
You will love you
And as you keep rising and rising and
Rising and rising to the highest
Manifestation of yourself,
Know that we've got your back
And I will always be falling in love with you.

The Conversation

1. How does the poem express the evolution of love from childhood to adulthood, and what does this say about the nature of love over time?

2. In what ways does the poem celebrate the roles and contributions of women in shaping individual and collective destinies?

3. How does the poet blend personal memories with broader societal roles to convey the multifaceted nature of women in our lives?

WHEN WE FLY

Can I fly with you as you spread your wings in the air like a beautiful butterfly to faraway places, bringing hope and care?

Can you fly with me as I strive to soar in solitude like the eagle to unknown spaces to see if I can heal and love again and not despair?

Can we fly together to a dream that we can only create with each other where uncertain cloudy skies are our only cover?

Only time knows where our flight is destined to go or if we will even try

So we both sigh and say, "Let us pray and see if today is our day."

I hear you whisper that maybe our only way is to take off in flight and stop this internal fight and go ahead and just spread our wings as we both dare to fly free.

The Conversation

1. How does the imagery of flight symbolize both personal healing and the potential for shared growth?
2. In what ways does the poem explore the balance between solitude and companionship in the pursuit of freedom?
3. How does the poet use nature and the skies to evoke a sense of possibility and transcendence?

In Gratitude

Thank you to the individuals who have poured into my life and helped bring *Cool Fire: A Black Man's Poetic Odyssey* to life. Writing this book has been a journey filled with love, lessons learned, legacy, and the power of words and images to inspire, transform, heal, and bring hope. As a person of faith, I believe that we are divinely created and have been blessed with the power to create, love, and live a life of meaning. I'm thankful every day for the gift of creativity and the opportunity to live with purpose.

To my ancestors—your courage and sacrifice are woven into every word I write. Your presence remains my guiding light. Your resilience and sacrifices laid the foundation for every step I take; I honor you. Specifically, to my first ancestor who landed in America and had the faith and fortitude to live despite whatever challenges came your way— thank you for instilling a spirit of resilience in me.

To my grandparents, who were instrumental in my having the opportunity to experience the joys of childhood. To my paternal grandparents, James and Lucy Dortch—your North Carolina home was a summer sanctuary of simplicity that allowed me to see the stars shine at night, to know the taste of fresh spring water, to feed the farm animals, and to learn to enjoy the fresh breath of nature. To my maternal grandparents, Henry and Thelma Towns—you instilled a spirit of belief and dreaming in me.

Granny, thank you for giving me the blank cardboard from your stocking packages, a pencil, a pen, and for encouraging me to create— and always making room for me at the table to read, pray, or listen to your stories. Granddaddy, thank you for instilling in me a love of history and storytelling as we rode the city and you shared stories of our native city with me. Your whispers of wisdom and strength echo through these pages.

Robert L. Dortch, Jr.

To my family—my parents and my brothers. To my father, Mr. Preacherman—thank you for your faithful spirit. I remember as a child looking into your bedroom and seeing you on your knees by the side of the bed, eyes closed, head bowed, and hands together, saying a prayer before you would start your day.

Thanks to my mother, Mrs. Ersey, for instilling in me the spirit of reading and learning. I used to go through your books, packed away in your childhood bedroom, and discovered Richard Wright, Maya Angelou, Langston Hughes, Alex Haley, and many others. I read every day because of you. You are one smart lady.

To my brothers, Reginald and Jeffrey, and my bonus sister, Cynthia—thank you for making childhood memories together. To my two big cousins, Evette and Peturla—I admire you both so much. Thank you for always allowing me to be me, even when I was the annoying little cousin who gave your dolls a haircut.

To my sons, Malcolm and Solomon—I am so proud to be your father and to witness you grow into beautiful men and human beings who care and love your family with kindness, humor, and compassion. You challenge and call me to be a better human being.

To the Rogers, Livingstons, Womacks, and Robinsons—thanks for making me a part of your family.

To Union Baptist Church—thank you for always allowing me a sacred space to grow, to explore my faith, to question tradition, to define my theology, and to always welcome me back home with love.

To those who have dared and chosen to love me—from my first elementary school crush to my first love, to the women who love and have loved me to this moment—thank you for always being my anchor of inspiration, my compass, my muse, my mirror, and my safe place to dream in smiles, tears, passion, and purpose. I am endlessly grateful for your love and unwavering support.

Thank you to all the brothers in my life who model humanity and masculinity through love, humor, and presence. To my Alpha Phi Alpha frat brothers from Xi Delta at James Madison University and the Rho Iota Chapter, my Mass Production line brothers from Spring '87, and my Ujima Legacy Fund brothers—thank you for standing with me, holding me accountable, and always showing up in love. Thank you for your encouragement and belief in a bigger vision for us, especially when the days are long, outcomes uncertain, responsibilities call—and yet you make time to listen to a brother pontificate, question, debate, and dream about a better world for us, those we love, our children, our families, and our communities.

To all the educators who supported my continuous learning journey—from Blackwell Elementary School, Westover Middle School, Falling Creek Middle School, Meadowbrook High School, James Madison University, the Samuel D. Proctor School of Theology at Virginia Union University, and beyond. Special shout-out to Dr. Ronald Carey, Coach Dave Cathers, Forest Parker, Dr. Byron Bullock, and Dr. Charles Pringle, who were instrumental in my becoming a first-generation college graduate.

To Dr. John W. Kinney and my STVU professors and classmates, thanks for creating a space for me to discover my authentic theological voice and for us to embark on the journey to the land of our beginning, West Africa. To Mrs. Ella Grimes, thanks for being our seminary mother.

To the creative collaborators of *Cool Fire*—your creativity and faith in me have made ideas tangible and beautiful. To everyone who contributed your time, talent, and energy to bring this book to life, you have been such an important part of this process.

To the graphic designer and editor, Jessica Tilles—I am grateful for your precision, patience, strategy, design, and editorial brilliance, as well as all the ways you have helped breathe life into this project. To David Landis—for the cover design and your ability to bring life to my thoughts and embrace my duality into a cover that compels readers to want to look inside.

To Gigi Amateau, thank you for the early morning coffee conversations and for encouraging me to write and connecting me with those who could offer guidance.

To Stacy Hawkins Adams—my sister and writing coach—thank you for challenging me to be a disciplined writer, to write when I am inspired and even when I am not, because that's what writers do.

To Bonnie Newman Davis—thank you, and BND, for sponsoring and supporting my early projects by creating a space for me to share my story of being a Black man and summiting Kilimanjaro with multiple audiences.

To Kimberly Wilson—thank you for being "FREE," for your presence and support, for believing in me, for encouraging me behind the scenes, and constantly challenging me to open up and share my story through preaching, poetry, and photography.

To Kelli Lemon—thank you for offering Urban Hang Suite as a canvas and platform in 2020 to host my first photo exhibits.

To Laura Gerald—thank you for inspiring me to grow as a leader and for taking time from your busy schedule to read the first draft of *Cool Fire* in its entirety and offer insightful, honest feedback on why it was good and how it could be better. Thank you for challenging me to see the world differently and more deeply.

To Joeffrey Trimmingham—thank you for letting me share some of my poetry during our dinner conversations.

To Kym Grinnage—thank you for saying yes, for supporting many of my ideas, podcasts, and events, and for inviting me to share my stories with the broader community through your platforms.

To Marlene Paul—thank you for encouraging me to attend open mic nights hosted by Lorna Pinckney (RIP) and for pushing me to share my poetry with the world.

To Tracey Wiley—thank you for *Rainmaker*, for your spirit of faith, for your public relations guidance throughout this process, and for offering ideas of how the impossible could become possible.

To Marland Buckner—thank you for the thought-provoking and profound conversations throughout the years that have stretched my intellectual capacity and for your feedback on the work.

To Q Martin—thank you for being available and saying yes to supporting the *Cool Fire* experience.

To Otis Jones and Elisha Burke—you may not realize how often I remember your voices after an event, encouraging me to write a book.

To Karen Rogers—you believed in me many years ago and hired me for my first art project. The rest is history. Thank you, and thank you to Nexus Digital for your consistent thought leadership, friendship, and support throughout the years. You have been instrumental in helping me convey my vision of telling and sharing stories to create a more beautiful and blessed world—not just for some, but for all people.

To the elders and poets who came before me—thank you for your guidance, your truth, and your courage to write words that challenged systems, defied stereotypes, spoke truth to power with love, moved mountains, and changed the world.

Thanks to everyone who prayed and believed in me and this project, for your commitment to excellence, and for investing your time, love, talent, support, and encouragement to help bring *Cool Fire* to life.

Thank you, readers, for journeying with me through this collection. May these poems and photographs ignite and inspire something within you, as they have within me.

Finally, to the spirit that breathes life into all things—thank you for giving me the courage to dream and the passion to create.

With gratitude and love,

Robert L. Dortch, Jr.

About the Author

Robert L. Dortch, Jr. is a poetic and prophetic voice, an emerging photographer, and a creative force for good. A native of Richmond, Virginia, Robert is the eldest son of Ersell and Robert Dortch, Sr., and the grandson of Henry and Thelma Towns and James and Lucy Dortch. He is the father of two sons.

Robert is the founder and principal of Jordan/Sydnor Innovation Group, a strategic coaching and consulting firm focused on helping people and organizations thrive through innovation, change, and courageous leadership. His career as an executive leader spans more than 25 years across the philanthropic, nonprofit, faith-based, and business sectors, where he has stewarded millions in investments to advance community impact and wellness. At the governance level, he has served on numerous boards, including as Chair of the Board of Trustees for Philanthropy Southeast, one of the largest Philanthropic Serving Organizations(PSOs) in the nation.

A sought-after speaker, facilitator, and executive coach, Robert has reached national and international audiences with messages of leadership, resilience, faith, and transformation. He is the author of Adventures in Leadership: A 30-Day Quest to Elevate Your Leadership & Life and the co-founder of the Ujima Legacy Fund, one of the nation's leading Black-led giving circles.

Robert's creative work blends photography and poetry to tell stories of love, faith, courage, and beauty—capturing everyday moments through the lens of an African American man living with purpose. He was Executive Producer of the African American Trailblazers educational series and documentary, which aired nationally on PBS stations.

A lifelong learner and adventurer, Robert holds a B.B.A. from James Madison University (with a concentration in Human Resource Management), an M.Div. from the Samuel D. Proctor School of Theology at Virginia Union University, an executive coaching certification from Georgetown University, and a Diversity & Inclusion certification from Cornell University. He's received numerous honors, which include being recognized as a distinguished alumnus of Chesterfield County Public Schools and receiving the 2025 Ronald E. Carrier Alumni Achievement Award from James Madison University. He has completed three marathons, summited Mount Kilimanjaro, and finds joy in journaling, hiking, and baking.

Robert's mission is simple yet profound: to be a creative force for good and to create spaces where all people can live lives of wellness, meaning, and purpose.

www.ingramcontent.com/pod-product-compliance
Lightning Source LLC
Chambersburg PA
CBHW042300090526
44582CB00019B/201/J